Come Rain, Come Shine

Come Rain, Come Shine

poems by

Jack B. Bedell

Texas Review Press
Huntsville, Texas
A Member of the Texas A&M Press Consortium

FIRST EDITION, 2006

Cover Art: Rolland Golden, *Spring Rain in the Delta*, courtesy of the artist.

Author's Photo: Claude Levet

Requests for permission to reproduce material from this work should be sent to:

> Texas Review Press
> English Department
> Sam Houston State University
> P.O. Box 2146
> Huntsville, TX 77341-2146

Library of Congress Cataloging-in-Publication Data
Bedell, Jack, 1966-
  Come rain, come shine / by Jack B. Bedell.-- 1st ed.
    p. cm.
  ISBN 1-881515-86-9 (alk. paper) -- ISBN 1-881515-87-7 (pbk. : alk. paper)
  1. Louisiana--Poetry. 2. Cajuns--Poetry. I. Title.
  PS3552.E2877C66 2006
  811'.54--dc22
                         2005023756

For the memory of Jim Whitehead,
whose voice I hear before every word I write,

and

For Beth, Jack, and Samuel,
without whom none of these poems would be possible.

Narrative arises with the recognition we are bearers of history.

Alan Shapiro

When I write about living in that privileged place, since it was
beautiful and remains so, I feel moved to show the reality of life there,
its urgency and validity.

Mark Jarman

Contents

Acknowledgments

My deepest gratitude to the editors in whose journals these poems originally appeared:

Aethlon, "If You Want to Catch the Big Fish You Got to Use the Big Lure"; *Connecticut Review*, "At the Lighthouse," "Camp at Night," "Come Rain or Come Shine," "Dead Heron," "Les Mains Du Bon Dieu," "Old Pelican"; *Hudson Review*, "Fête de la Roulaison," "The Last Supper," "One Morning, Over Dove"; *Paterson Literary Review*, "Après la Roulaison," "Chari Vari de Jean Lirette," "Loup Garou"; *Southeast Review*, "Fall, Batfishing," "Left in Bed" (as "Anniversary Still Life"), "Summer, Handfishing," "The Vegetarian Warms Up"; *Southern Review*, "L'avalasse"; *Texas Review*, "The Novice"

Come Rain, Come Shine

I

Fête de la Roulaison

All morning cane trucks have driven into the mill
bringing the last stalks for the grinding. The cutters

have burned the fields from outside in and wait
at the edges, guns turned towards rabbits

for the stew. The children run behind the flames,
ruddy as sky from playing too close to ground.

The women raise tables in the clearing, spread
white cloths for the feast. Last year's dresses

hang on them, bland from the wash and begging
for the breeze to stir someplace close enough

to remind them winter is coming and this year's cane
will bring brand-new dresses and food from town.

Après la Roulaison

The young groom wakes to stars and October chill
to find a trail of bedclothes disappearing
into the children's cane. There's nothing left
of the festival, save the smoke that lingers
above the burned fields. The cane's been pressed,
the trucks readied for the trip to town.

Here and there nighthawks skim the clearing
for mice. There's no other movement
above the rows as he gathers wood for the fire.
His tries to think of the evening they've just passed
alone, the lines of her back beneath the moon,
the hope of money this year's cane will bring,

but cannot keep his mind from what waits for her
between the stalks—snakes left from summer,
sinkholes yawning for her legs, blades
left carelessly about. He does not blink
until the cane parts, releasing her to the clearing
naked and smiling, stronger than he knew.

In the fire's glow he sees a spider web
stretched across her stomach, hip to hip,
the shine of her skin against the night, her eyes
closing slowly with each step toward him.

Next year's growth surrounds them in the dark,
and morning holds its breath across the fields.

Burn to New

Our new year doesn't start with the sweet smell
of white sugar in sparkly china bowls here,
but the sour, bagasse smell of *cannes brulée*,
the cane trash burning from the stalks before harvest.
To ready the cane for grinding at the mill,
the old men ease themselves to the center of the field
with boards to stamp the stalks and torches for the blaze.

They clear what space they need and set the leaves
afire, returning to the edge of the old growth
where the young men wait with shotguns raised, aiming
for whatever's made its home in the cane, hoping
to fill their pots with rabbit, coon, and dove
for the *fête* that night, knowing the stew would run thin
each year without this burn. They blink their eyes
against the sting and shoot as true as they can.

The guns sound before the smoke rises
high enough for the women at the mill
to see it and ready the tables with white cloths.
In less than two hours the fire will have done its share,
leaving the cane stalks there for the taking,
stripped and ready for the *roulaison*,
the field black with the promise of money and market.

The real work of cutting and binding can rest
until tomorrow's sun when stomachs are full
and there's nothing left of this fire save its smell.
While this dusk lasts, our children will play in the smoke
just outside the flame's hungry mouth.
Cattle and the rest of us wait patiently
near the fenceline for the heat's slow approach,
the rich winter air just on the other side.

Fête de la Quémande

Every family on the plain wakes
Fat Tuesday to the sound of the Capitaine's hooves
at its gate. His troupe waits on horseback, bursting

with color and mischief in the morning sun,
their robes and hats dyed the reddest red,
their masks painted with rosy cheeks and mustaches.

This Mardi Gras runs from house to house, singing
at each window for an invitation
to dismount. The Capitaine will ride alone

to each door with his white flag and whip,
the peacemaker and keeper of the code,
asking permission for his men to start their begging.

They will spill from their horses into the grass, rolling
over each other in a boil of demands,
shining the men's shoes and kissing the hands

of all women foolish enough to step outside.
If they are given rice to go away,
they want a chicken for the night's gumbo.

If given onions, they'll slap the house's glass
until the birds are released. They'll only stop
when the Capitaine decides their work is done

or has gone too far in its jest. He keeps their goals
in mind—to gather enough to feed everyone
this feast before Lent, to see the sun off safely.

Tonight, his men will dance like earth and fire
knowing tomorrow everything will burn
to ash and six weeks of silent, patient love.

Paqueing Eggs at Easter

As soon as the sun is up, the old women come
with baskets full of colored eggs to paque.
They knock on every door, offering
the brightest ones to tap small end to end.

They always start with easy paques, losing
the eggs they know will crack with any peck,
until their loss is pitiful enough
to change the trade to fresh eggs for those cracked.

It's then they'll reach for their dullest egg, a guinea
dyed so gray it could easily be a stone.
No matter how they're struck, small end or large,
these eggs don't break. The women fill their baskets

door by door, and leave to start the day's work.
By the time morning mass has ended, their ovens
swell with small deceits, the white shells gone,
each yolk a cross bun for the evening feast.

Chari Vari de Jean Lirette

At dusk they come in force, a *coup de mains*.
The town brings a noise he knows in his chest.
With copper pots and spoons they raise the voice
of his wife, gone to ground not seven months.

She was a Martin and of the place. Her things
stare down from every wall and cast shadows
across his new love, all red hair and skin
so white she glows against their Parisian bed.

He knows this crowd will not be satisfied
with bread and strawberry wine. They've come for the joy
of waking his conscience, bringing the old stares
of his wife's kin straight into the room.

Some want the wedding china they bought with sweat
to chip and fall from the cabinet. Some want
the furniture they finished to lose its stain
and break apart into scrapwood on the floor.

Most, though, would love to see him lose
his breath and die atop this teenage bride,
too soon off the boat to have met any of them,
too sweet to know why they have come to call.

Pas des Gothes

Because she is a girl and cannot play
the game, she always asks to make the marks.
She pulls the roosters' shapes from hardwood,
holding each cypress plank between her legs
to shave against the grain with her two-handled knife.

Her birds are tall and fat, their soft hearts masked
under thick coats of red porch paint, their eyes
slanted and smiling like her own each time
the horsemen fail to shoot them through. The love
she's put into each brush stroke makes her wood

too much for their .22 shot. She cannot help
but grin as the boys pass, their rifles low
and hanging closer to ground each time they hear
the whistles from the fathers' gallery,
her roosters high and whole in the field till dusk.

Loup Garou

Some nights a shadow bends the sugar cane
        towards the back porch, and what wind there is
                carries a scent that starts the dog to grumbling.

It doesn't matter that all the locks are latched
        and all the knives are put away. The moon
                has risen over the fields, and coons and treefrogs

press their bellies against cypress and keep quiet.
        These are nights mothers warn their children
                to keep hands and feet over the mattress;

the Loup Garou is coming for their fingers and toes.
        It doesn't have to come as the wolf, or fog.
                It could easily be the blue heron creeping

just behind the children's cane, or the nighthawk
        razing each row for field mice. Any light-footed shape
                can bring it close enough to make frissons.

And nothing, not even an infant's calm breath,
        can keep it back, until the sun climbs
                over the cane and burns its eyes away.

Ouaouaron

Spring nights, in the calm between rains,
the bullfrogs in the tranasse beside our house

sing the song of themselves, so deep
and relentless the dog presses her nose

to the backdoor glass and whines.
I always feel I should wake my sons,

drag them across the wet grass
to see such desperate love, but know

somewhere deep in my chest each step
we'd take toward it would only serve

to chase it farther away into the dark,
stilled and resonant with desire.

L'avalasse

The old women of our parish
say such rain, *l'avalasse*,
throws sheets of sleep across your house
to wash away whatever burden
the day has brought. They walk outside
in their nightgowns as soon as the bullfrogs
stiffen in the ditch and hunker down,
believing the water will cleanse them of aches
and lighten the weight their years have built.

It's enough for me to step to the porch
with the dog to watch the backyard fill.
Inside, my wife and boys draw close
and breathe with such peace the house almost glows.
Their sleep is thick and well-deserved.
There's nothing worth waking them for
as long as this storm holds us to its heart.
I know the dreams they share will be enough
to keep us afloat when morning comes.

Outside, a murder of crows has landed
pecking its way through the mess this rain
has washed off our house into the grass.
Somewhere, the old women are bathing,
their lesson in the water coming down—

no matter how it pounds, this rain
will not outlast Noah's. Our land
is thirstier than his, our sins
much easier to wash away.

II

Les Mains du Bon Dieu

(after a line in Daigrepont's Cajun Spiritual)
                              —for my uncle, Ray Rougeau

The last word I can picture you saying to me
was "Faith." It sticks because you were never a man
people would call talkative, even before
the nurses wrote you down as unresponsive,
before they took your staring at the cracks
in the white walls of your room as some kind of loss.
They see in your eyes a man who would hand them back
anything they gave you without sign of recognition,
but every time you rest your eyes from the wall
to meet mine we are together on a popelier dock
in early fall, the sky flat-grey on the water.
A run of bull red has knocked the conversation
out of us, turning it all into cast and reel—
backbone and shoulders. The fish are so big
the only thing they hit is small crab
on shad rigs. We've already filled the boat
to near sinking, so you leave me there on the dock
to ride out our luck while you bring the first load
back to the camp to ice down. Alone, I live
a twelve-year-old's dream: every time I cast
I land a big one to pile on the dock as testament
to the day. It is more than I can handle, more

than we deserve, but I keep pulling them in.
You return in time to see my rod
arc and the line give more than it has all day.
You watch me fight this monster patiently
and load the boat again. Almost by script,
just when I want to fold, the fish runs
straight at us, between the pylons under the dock.
With no sign or pause you take the rod from my hand
and toss it into the water. It is all I can do
not to follow it, a rig worth more allowances
than I can imagine lost for one fish
in a pile of one hundred just like it. You pull me near
and whisper the word mostly to yourself. Your eyes
stare calmly at something just below the surface
I can not make out. When the redfish comes around
to make its last run at the gulf, the rod follows
as if delivered by the hands of God.
In a single motion you catch it up
and pass it to me to finish out the day.
Before my line breaks and your stare returns
to the wall, I have a sense of what you mean:
Mettez votre vie dans les mains du Bon Dieu.

Summer, Handfishing

My uncle's rules were simple enough.
Leave your boots behind at the truck,
a bare sole the difference
between a small cut on the foot
and the real pain of angry metal
forced straight up through a shoe.
Approach everything with care,
palms down, fingers out.
Live by every decision—
nothing grabbed wants to be,
so use your hands with forceful purpose.
 And just in case you grab something
more decisive than you, before
it grabs you back, let it go.

Fall, Batfishing

It all started as easily as the idea
of gravity—a football thrown at dusk
between low pines, the flutter that tracked it
almost to the ground, then the equation.

One boy went for the apple, the other the knife.
I was sent for my Zebco 808
because my house was closest and I moved
slow enough my mother never asked.

Before any of us could reason right from wrong,
before our mothers' fear of rabies intruded,
the apple was on the hook and sailing up
into the trees.
                        What bit offered no fight.
It joined the dead weight of the apple and fell
to the street as helpless as a choupique born
without bones.
                        Having landed a creature
as alien to us as snow, we could not help
but scratch ourselves and gather. The parts of it
that showed—the vicious teeth and see-through wings—
should never have seen our flashlight's beam.

The vision of it chased all of us back home
without even a poke of the knife or a taunt
for the thing. We left it there sprawled in the street.
It didn't seem as hurried as you'd think,
nor as bitter at our sport as I would be.

Years later, alone in my college library,
I learned bats must fall into flight and know
nothing of the severity of ground.

If You Want to Catch the Big Fish
You Got to Use the Big Lure

—for Clay Mixon

When the big net's already in the water
and the line snaps, no boat's got enough room
for those of us holding drinks and not poles.
I had seen the thing. Hell, we had all seen it,
but that just makes it worse. It's safe to say
everything we'll ever know about loss
is at the end of that curling twine Clay's holding.
I swear when he drew back nothing, the sun ran
for home and beavers and bullfrogs froze solid,
so how can I tell him that this is no sign
of Calvinistic unworthiness, that he
is not some Puritan preacher whose house burnt down
from God's spite, that his woman won't pack up
and go as soon as we hit the dock? He fought
the good fight with this beast, played when he had to,
yanked and cursed, too, but now he's locked
in a land of "shoulda," where his fish has turned
"alternative" down by the cypress stump,
that big Arkansas Tuna lure hanging
from his pierced lip. His is a pain that swells
the more we tell it, the more we conjure up
that six-pounder rolling over toward home.

Because he is my friend, I'll wait until supper
to tell him what I know—that something bigger
and far more vicious is holed up at the bottom
of that pond growing by the minute to fit his lure.

The Vegetarian Warms Up to the Dance Floor
At Fred's Lounge, Mamou, Louisiana

—for Tim and Winborne

A.M. and the bar's already full of men
who'll stand in a line for only two things:
Schlitz beer and blonde women. The vegetarian
is neither. She's skinny and white as snow peaks,
all dark hair and lips sipping Lite beer.
When the owner, Tante Sue, offers her the tray
of boudin sausage she shakes her head and cringes,
orders a green salad with vinaigrette.
At this, Tante Sue laughs her cigarette-
and-peach-Schnaaps laugh and wades into the crowd.

The band is on a two-step and the floor
is full of work-tanned men in their best jeans
and pearl-button shirts, closer to each other
than they'd ever be on a week day, pulling
whatever tourist woman who'll go for it
into the mix. The vegetarian is amazed
their caps stay on, pinching as little head
as they do way up on the crown like that.
She lags back and starts to dismiss it all
as a scene from some dumb Cajun joke

when T-Gautreaux whisks her into the boil
of dancers. There's not enough room to embarrass herself
on this floor, so she falls straight into the rhythm
of his chicken limp and prays for the song to end.
But something about the force of his hand on her back,
the rasp in the old accordianist's voice, or the orgy
of tempo kicked up by the triangle player stirs her.
And even though this isn't the conversion
a slab of ribeye would cause, it is enough
to raise some color into her rigid face.

Turtle Cove Suite

—Lake Manchac Observatory, 1999

I. Old Pelican

The pelican presides at the end of the dock
not stirring an inch as we unload our bags
and go about the business of settling
into the camp. Around him, May
is in high gear. The grasshoppers mate
on everything, crawl mechanically
from love to love. Garfish run
in schools beside the dock chasing
shad and mullet. The air is alive
with horsefly and mosquito hawk,
but not pelican. The old guy
bides his time keeping one eye
on us, the other on the sun
as it stretches across the water toward dusk.
No loud talk of art or bang
of Samsonite can break his pace.
He puts no truck in hotdog buns
or minnows offered at his feet,
has no fear of rubber toys
bounced his way. It's not until,
bored, we file into the house,

he turns himself to face the wind,
spreads his wings against the dying sun,
and flies off toward the lighthouse
that borders our horizon.

II. At the Lighthouse

In early May, when rain is too far off
to comfort us and any breeze is enough
to stir the reeds, to light the sweat on our faces
and pull them toward the sun, you've come to me.
I did not think you'd meet me here where ground
falls into the persistence of the lake.
It's a place where water and space restrict you.
You've come to see what dance is possible
in hipboots. I have come to talk of sunsets,
pelicans, and fundraisers for this crooked beacon.
Boaters on the Pass must think it strange
to see us standing here with our heads bowed
in silence, nary a net or pole in sight.
The lighthouse, falling into the water as it is,
offers little explanation to them.

III. Camp at Night

We lose each other's face by candlelight
to chase away the swarm of gnats that grows
toward anything electrical.
The years of this place bear down on us in darkness
board by board. Somewhere in the shadows
President Roosevelt's ghost leans his .10 gauge
against the brick fireplace and strides to the window
to check on his dogs, deep in lemon grass
and straining at their ties after lightning bugs.
Cicadas swell in the trees and the camp settles
room by room. Out front, the porch creaks
with ninety years of hunters and scientists.
Under the camp, the heads of rattlesnakes
and alligators stew in specimen jars.
Crawfish and crab traps wait on the dock.
Night grows around everything. Beyond the camp,
the dark is as it has always been—pure space.
There is only the feel of heat and watered air,
a life older than we can possibly know.

Dead Heron

It startles me to find it pinned to barbed wire
on the edge of some pasture in southwest Arkansas
so far from water it could only have been mistaken.
Its blue feathers lift in the wind;
its head bends sideways languidly, a sketch
from Audubon's notebook. Nothing in the field
seems to welcome it.
                          Back home, these birds
are ancestors gliding across the salt marsh
between cypress knots, spearing mullet
and spreading into the summer wind for their mates.
They move toward the sky with sincerity.

Here, there is no dignity in its decay—
ants eating its grace from inside out,
hornets and beetles burrowing into it.
Whatever ghost its tendons held in life
must surely find it shameful suspended on land,
dry and falling to earth piece by piece.

Only a visitor myself, it is
the least I can do to pry it down and keep it
with my gear until I can set it free to glide
on the first river I come to.

White Letters, Black Roofs

—for Clark Byers, 1915-2004

Somewhere between the highway and a barn
in need of paint, the promise of his day
bloomed. His offer to the farmer was plain—
fresh paint, Rock City bath mats, thermometers,
or a week's pay if the roof was too clear a shot
for cars driving by. Nine hundred times he stood
at the edge of that field loaded down with paint,
chalk, brushes, rope, and hours of light.

Each step across the grass brought something new
to the words he drew for thirty years. Some days
brought bulls who wouldn't give him the foot he needed
to pass by, and had to be coaxed with sweet corn or salt.
Some days brought rattlesnakes and sinkholes to juke.
Some days brought lightning or a slippery roof,
and then he'd have to hum church songs to quiet
his heart enough to make it through the day.

No matter the size of the barn, two coats of red paint
hit the walls before he'd take his biscuits and coffee.
He always ate on the roof so he could figure
the best spot to place his sign, and check
how many cars passed by to see it done.

By mid-afternoon, he'd have the roof black
and would set to drawing all eleven letters
by hand, first with chalk, and then white paint.

He stood on top of barns from Michigan
to Florida, sometimes able to see
the flowers of seven states from one perch,
other times struggling to see past his nose
on foggy mountaintops, but always he had
the truth of white letters on black roofs,
the pride of his steady hand that urged us all
to See Rock City before the day had closed.

The Novice

—Ursuline Convent, 1799

Hers is the flat gaze of a second-year wife
whose husband has gone hunting for the winter
leaving her the lonely chores of devotion,
the endless days of loving preparation
for His uncertain return. The bloom she felt
as a newlywed has slowly been replaced
by girlish dreams of trappers' sons and pralines,
of mirrors and the long, black hair she braided
until her arms grew sore. In her doorless room
she remembers that ache scrubbing the floorboards
to a glass shine beneath the approving eyes
of her Holy Sisters who pass in silence
straightening the images of the scourged Christ
that hang on every wall. What passes for love
is just as close as she can get to seeing
a reflection of herself. When the halls calm
she stands beneath the window's light admiring
her body as the men have done at market.
In the floor's dull pane, she frees her hands to haunt
her milk-white skin, to skim its topography.
She allows herself a young wife's pout and stoops
for one last glimpse of her lips before the floor
dries and she goes about dressing for supper.

One Morning, Over Dove

My wife is not afraid of blood
or knives. She's spent all morning cleaning
the doves Brother and I swept
from the soy bean fields beside our land.

She scrapes the hearts and livers out
with her fingers into a bowl and piles
the rest of the birds onto the table.
By the time I step out back to stow

the shotguns, she's already filled a pail
with meat for the week's stew and wants
to talk of love and children and time.
The whole while she builds a stain

on her forehead, brushing away a hair
that interrupts important points
of room temperatures and ovulations.
I wipe down my .20 gauge

and wonder at the tenderness
she holds in her voice while elbow-deep
in gore. The space between her words
and mine is enough to register

desire, and more than enough for her
to clean two doves, reaching her fingers
into their chests, popping the meat
out with a subtle snap.

The Last Supper

Because my wife's the kind of woman
who'd rather see a prison museum
than tour the oldest home in Huntsville,
I find myself in rows of homemade pistols
forged from pipe, shieves filed down from spoons,
and knives made from angle-iron
splayed like Christmas trees to go in easy,
come out like a world of hurt.

The walls around are plastered with oddments:
rodeo flyers, a letter from Clyde Barker
to Henry Ford praising his V-8,
a century of newsclippings announcing riots,
executions, politicians' visits,
craft shows, and new construction—
simple enough for the prison's resume.

A life-sized cell and Old Sparky
frame the whole experience.
The distance between the two could never be enough
for a man who knows the day he's going to die.
I can't wrap my mind around the deliberation
it would take to button my shirt for the last time
or to order my last meal prepared fire hot
and in enough bowls so none of it would touch.

The weight of a man's choices bears down on me
in the menu cards taped to the glass,
and nothing I could choose would lend faith
or direction enough to make Death close up shop
and shuffle back down the hall.

My wife slips in behind me to study scene
as quiet as a warden in the witness box.
"Soft-shelled crabs," she says into my ear.
"I wouldn't even have to think about it."

My Wife Bathing

—2.7.01

She spends an hour in slow curve
tracing and retracing the bend of elbow,
the back of knee. A long day
frets off her into the water
with soaps and oils, steam rising
toward acceptance of its close.
Her hands hover constantly
stirring her thoughts from one end
of the tub to the other, painting release
across her body. Slow-eyed and smiling
she turns to her stomach, the slope of her back
and her shoulders spreading into the heat.
Around her, our house is still.
Even the air waits for her to rise
out of her joy and into the room—
refreshed, clean, and more beautiful
than anything I have ever known.

Left in Bed

—for Beth

This first morning of our second year
the squirrels in our yard have set up shop
as they always do—two feet
from the neighbor dog, torturing him
into his wake-up calls, stirring you
to roll toward me in the sunlight.

For a while I have your face
free of all lines and cares.
This is how I hold you in my dreams,
all cheekbone and soft shoulders,
breathing carefully as the blue jays
outside our bedroom jump from branch to branch.

Without the day-born chide of bill or chore
every part of you becomes the future—
the hands that will hustle our children to school,
the back that will stretch to leave beignet dough
to rise on the fridge for our Sunday meal,
the legs that will share the retirement quilt
with mine when I'm all give-out.

But you don't have to become art
to hunger me, nor do I need
metaphor to see you as love.
It is enough to have you here
left in bed when I rise for work,
for you to slide without so much as a yawn
into the space my body leaves.

Son

—12.20.02

I will never have words for how your every move
stirs inside of me, so these will have to do:

I have listened to you breathe for 365 days
and still cannot keep from putting my hand on your chest

to feel it rise as you sleep, head tilted up,
lips parted as if tasting something too beautiful

for this world. Most nights the dog wakes me to go out,
and I pass the time in your room until she begs back in

making sure you are warm and have something soft
near your face to keep your dreams safe and light.

I wonder how many more breaths it will take
before I can watch you run the yard and play

in the moonlight with the dog, how many dreams
will pass before I will have to beg you in

without your mother knowing you are barefoot
and awake, how many more times your turning

will pull me from sleep before I will know
you are safe on your own and can breathe without me.

Swordplay

Even at two, my son is relentless.
I plan my strategies at work
since he allows no time to change
into suitable gear, no chance
for limbering up old injuries.

As soon as I walk in the door
he chooses our weapons and sets the rules.
We usually begin with light sabers
and work our way back through the history
of blades, each with its own technique.

He grips his saber with two hands,
keeping his feet wide for sweeping strokes,
moving forward without fear
of my defenses. If I find his rhythm
he switches quickly to pirate's steel.

Always he hands me a matching sword,
smaller than his own if possible.
On the open sea, his footwork quickens
and his wrist takes on a lethal figure 8
that swings his blade from left to right

harboring violence and intent.
To slow his charge, I parry with questions—
Captain Jack, who do you love?
"Mommy, you scurvy dog."
Arrr Matey, how about Daddy?

"How about No" is the best I get
in return. I've sat in classrooms too long
not to sense where this is headed
symbolically, and often lose my focus
imagining how his blue eyes will glisten

as a man. But he always turns his back
at my lack of effort, and taunts me
by slapping my blade with his free hand
behind him, his eyes toward the window,
his feet planted and bored still.

No matter where our battles take us,
he ends them the same by drawing
a broadsword for which I have no foil.
I drop my mark and raise my hands
pleading, Not a fair fight.

Jean Lafitte at Bath

I put my son to bath the other night
and set about shaving for my next day's work.
His load of toys seemed random at first glance—
a few ships with crew, rubber alligators,
a treasure chest of Mardi Gras doubloons—
nothing worth breaking the comfort of lather and blade,
until I heard my mother in his voice.

He told himself the story of Jean Lafitte
in the same words my mother had used for me,
how the pirate sailed up Bayou Lafourche to hide
his treasure from the English navy, resting
only on moonlit nights, tying his ship
to the banks, his men pitching chicken parts
in all directions to draw the alligators
so no one could swim up on them as they slept.

He poured these words without taking a breath,
like the Frenchman's freedom meant something to us all,
like the victory of watching the English sails
wander aimlessly around Grand Isle
was our own treasure to share coin by coin.
He ordered his men to leave food and clothes
at every dock just to make it so.

I didn't even have to turn around
to feel the pirate's sunrise on my neck,
to see my son's blue eyes glisten at the shore
as the trappers' daughters stepped toward him, giggling,
his ship making its way to open waters,
that Frenchman's treasure safe and glimmering
as it fell straight from my mother's hands to his.

Come Rain or Come Shine

—2.7.03

This is a promise without boundary or sense
until the first night the baby wakes
every hour with a pain in his voice
that can only be soothed by his mother's breath
on his neck or the soft comfort of her rocking
from foot to foot in the dark; until days pass
without a single conversation about anything
except the baby's fever or sore mouth
or his eating or not eating or smiling or not smiling;
until sleep and quiet are your only desires.

And then comes the rainy morning when the baby sleeps
past nine, or the night he goes to sleep before ten;
when the bed is warm and touch is no dream
but something shared like a hot, slow-cooked meal
unrushed by crying or need; or that long moment
when a wife steps from the bath and is not mother
but a clenching in your chest that makes the day shine
enough for everyone in the house; and suddenly you know
the distance between the beginning of these words
and the blessing of love that will help you carry them out.

Notes

Fête de la Roulaison—the grinding festival celebrated just before the sugar cane goes to market

Bagasse—smelly refuse left over after grinding sugar cane

Canne brulée—burned sugar cane

Fête de la Quémande—begging festival celebrated in 17th century France, the root of our modern Courir du Mardi Gras in south Louisiana

Paqueing— an Acadian Easter ritual in which participants compete for boiled eggs by knocking them small end to small end. In some settlements, fresh eggs are substituted as prizes for the toughest eggs

Chari vari—hazing reserved in Cajun culture for widowers who remarry too soon

Coup de mains—collective activity or show of force

Pas des Gothes— a traditional Cajun game of marksmanship in which boys on horseback get one shot per pass to break wooden targets. Often the broken marks can be exchanged for real foul, making the game more than simple fun. Girls are forbidden to play

Loup Garou—Cajun name for werewolves or shapeshifters

Ouaouaron—Cajun word for bullfrog

L'avalasse—Cajun word for torrential rain

Mettez votre vie dans les mains du Bon Dieu—translates as, "Put your life in the hands of God."

About the Author

Jack B. Bedell's latest collections are *What Passes for Love* and *At the Bonehouse*, both published by Texas Review Press (a member of the Texas A&M Press Consortium) and *Greatest Hits* (Pudding House Press). His recent work appears in the *Southern Review, Hudson Review, Connecticut Review, Paterson Literary Review, Texas Review, Southeast Review*, and other journals. He is an Associate Professor of English and Coordinator of creative writing at Southeastern Louisiana University where he also edits *Louisiana Literature*, a nationally-recognized literary journal, and directs the Louisiana Literature Press. He and his wife Beth have two sons, Jack, Jr. and Samuel Eli, and one large Labrador, Mocha.